I0062176

INVERTED LEADERSHIP

A Framework for Growing Strong Organisations

Richard J Haley

Copyright © Richard J Haley 2025

All Rights Reserved

No part of this publication may be reproduced, distributed, or transmitted in any form or by any means, including photocopying, recording, or other electronic or mechanical methods, without the author's prior written permission, except in the case of brief quotations embodied in critical reviews and certain other non-commercial uses permitted by copyright law. For permission requests, please get in touch with the author.

Table of contents

Acknowledgement

Without seeking it, I was put into a senior leadership position at the ripe old age of 26. I have always respected people older than me, and whilst it felt quite natural to lead, I was very conscious of my young age leading people much older, more experienced, and more talented than I was at my old job. However, this wasn't my old job. This was a new responsibility.

I consider myself very fortunate to have had subsequent leaders in my career who were excellent, skilled, humble, low in ego, and great role models. I remember a particular example during a large automotive design project when a mistake made by my project management team ended up costing us many, many thousands of pounds.

I was expecting a rocket (or worse) from the Chairman of the business. Instead, he told me that he considered it his "school fees" that I would learn from it and be wiser to the circumstances if ever they arose again.

At 61 years old, I often muse over the people I learnt from over the years, and I am very grateful for the example and pathways they carved out, making my own journey easier to navigate. Although this book contains my thoughts, insights, and views, I feel it stands on the foundations of those who mentored, taught, and supported me throughout the years.

About the Author

Richard Haley has been professionally coaching and mentoring leaders since 2007, following 27 years in the automotive design industry. He is also a practitioner of Emotional Intelligence.

In addition to his own leadership skills, Richard possesses an unusual set of other highly developed talents – he is also an accomplished artist, musician, creative and producer. His original musical production *Love Beyond* that he created and co-wrote all the music for, has been performed in many large venues, including Wembley Arena in London.

He has been married for 39 years, has four children, and eight grandchildren so far.

INVERTED LEADERSHIP

A Framework for Growing Strong Organisations

Introduction

I was sitting in a London café with a client, discussing the challenges his company was facing. He was the CEO of a tech company and a creative thinker. The conversation steered toward growth – his challenges in growing the business, and the challenges within his people.

He sketched out his existing organisational chart on his notepad beginning with his name at the top, then everyone else cascading down the page. He began to run out of room for all the 'workers' at the bottom. As he turned the page to create more space, I glanced out the window and noticed a set of beautiful olive trees basking in the sun, each in its own massive, Mediterranean-styled pot.

They all had an old, sturdy trunk that supported a vibrant canopy of branches and leaves, each one reaching up and out, seeking the light. To me, it was as if the silvery leaves were dancing – enjoying their existence as part of the tree. Each of the gnarled trunks was very different, and you could tell that they had their own unique story.

In that moment, I remember thinking: the traditional style of organisation chart being created in front of me was inadequate and simply a chart of responsibility. I could see that if we approached it differently, it could become a framework designed for growth. Normally, these charts are just snapshots that very quickly become out of date, destined to sit in someone's drawer until the next reorganisation.

The Problem with Being the Star

If you're reading this book, chances are you're either leading an organisation or aspiring to do so. Perhaps you've noticed something isn't quite working in your current structure, or in the structures of others. Maybe your teams aren't as engaged as you'd like, or your middle managers seem stuck in a perpetual power struggle. Or possibly, like many leaders I've worked with, you're simply exhausted from trying to live up to the pressure of being the shining star at the top of your organisational Christmas tree.

Don't worry – you're not alone. I've seen the same patterns repeat themselves across hundreds of organisations. Leaders struggle to maintain control while trying to empower their teams. Middle managers find themselves caught between serving those above and supporting those below. Front-line workers feel disconnected from their organisation's purpose, while everyone wonders why change and growth are so hard to implement.

The root of these problems may lie not in our people or our processes, but in a historical structural model that now frames most of today's organisations.

I have been coaching and mentoring CEOs and Directors from various organisations for the last 17 years – businesses, charities and faith groups – and have observed many organisational cultures, some very successful, and others less so. I believe there is a better framework than the one we all inherited. One that is natural, enduring, inclusive, designed for growth, and above all, very, very proven!

We'll look at the traditional organisation chart, and briefly at the history of why we build organisations based on this framework. More excitingly, however, we will explore the opportunity for growth by designing our organisations around a framework more suited to the 21st-century worker – and beyond.

Nature's Blueprint for Growth

Trees have been successfully growing, adapting, and thriving since the dawn of our planet. They've cracked the code for sustainable growth, developing from tiny seeds into resilient structures that can last for thousands of years.

What's most amazing is their adaptability – trees flourish in every environment imaginable, from desert to rainforest, from mountain peak to City Street. However, while no two varieties are the same, their basic structure follows a time-tested design that has proven itself for millennia.

This natural design offers us a powerful model for today's organisations, particularly in an age where people are highly educated and informed. In a tree, the trunk doesn't lord over its branches – it supports them. The branches don't compete for the trunk's attention – they collaborate to distribute resources wisely. And the leaves? They're not at the bottom of some hierarchy – they're the crown of the whole operation.

As we'll see in the chapters ahead, this isn't just a convenient metaphor. Trees have solved many of the same challenges that modern organisations face: how to distribute resources effectively, how to adapt to changing conditions, how to support growth while maintaining stability, and how to create conditions where every part can thrive.

What You'll Find in This Book

We'll explore every aspect of our organisational tree. We'll discover how roots – those often-forgotten support systems keep everything stable. We'll examine how the trunk provides core stability, strength, and resource flow. We'll learn why branches need to focus on support rather than control, and understand the vital importance of leaves in organisational health.

We'll also discuss practical ways to implement this natural approach to a growing entity, and the kind of leadership it requires in order to thrive. I will also include lots of examples from my experiences of coaching leaders through the years (with made-up names to protect identities).

A Word of Warning

This book isn't about quick fixes or management fads. Just as you can't force a tree to grow overnight, transforming an organisation takes time, patience, and consistent care. What I'm proposing isn't just a reorganisation – it's a fundamental shift in how we think about leadership and organisational structure in today's environment.

If you're looking for ways to exert more control over your organisation, this probably isn't the book for you. However, if you're ready to explore a more natural, sustainable approach to leadership – one that could transform not just your organisation, but your entire experience of leading – then turn the page.

So whether you're a seasoned CEO or an emerging leader, I hope this book will challenge the way you think about your role and offer a roadmap to building an organisation that can thrive in the face of any challenge.

I am not a horticulturist of any kind. In fact, prior to my coaching practice, I spent 27 years in the automotive design and development business. I love great design in whatever form it takes. Think of this book as a design evolution of traditional organisational structure, following extensive market research, and using the best model out there. And yes, it is short – I like short books.

So let's embark together on this journey. Let's explore what organisations can learn from the amazing design of trees. Discover how to develop and nurture – not unnaturally from the top down, but naturally and sustainably from the roots up.

Welcome to the world of Inverted Leadership.

1

The Problem with Looking Down

The Meeting That Said It All

Picture this: its 9 a.m. on a Thursday. I have been brought in to help this national retailer. Twelve executives are sitting around a boardroom table. Jade, the CEO, is standing at the whiteboard, marker in hand.

"Right," she says with forced enthusiasm, "let's map out our new structure."

What happens next is a scene I've witnessed many times. In an instant, Jade draws a box at the top of the board and writes her title in it. Then come the division heads, then their departments. Then more slowly, their teams – accompanied by an argument about dotted lines or questions like, "Can they report to two people?"

Discussions take place to try and distribute functions more evenly, because "you cannot have more than seven people report to anyone," says the person known to the room for reading books on leadership and self-development.

There is then a discussion about where the 'oddball' should sit – the person with unique skills that the business needs, but who has a personality no one wants to inherit.

Until finally – almost as an afterthought and in much smaller writing because there is little room left – the frontline workers appear at the bottom of the board. There is no discussion about them.

Sound familiar?

By the time Jade puts the cap back on her marker, the board looks powerful, deliberate, with her shining as the star at the top. Everyone nods approvingly. After all, this is how organisations are supposed to look, right?

Knowing Jade – and, in fact, many other Principal Leaders I have helped – they don't always want to be seen as the shining star at the top that everyone bows down to. The expectations of this starring role can sometimes be unhelpful. For example, the strong, gifted introverted leader having to have their name up in lights and be expected to give inspirational speeches all of the time.

These everyday organisational charts fail to inspire. I have seen them inflate the egos of upper management. I have seen them deflate the value of the workers near the bottom. I have seen them generally be out of date – and most often hidden away or "on the system somewhere." They usually only get resurrected when the next big change in the organisation is being considered.

Why are we looking to change this structure?

If you're a leader, you might be experiencing some warning signs right now that perhaps things aren't flowing out of a brilliantly designed framework. For example:

The Communication Cascade

You carefully craft a message at the top, send it down through the ranks, and by the time it reaches the front line, it has lost its clarity and meaning – and gained a few extra unhelpful nuances. Your crystal-clear vision has somehow transformed into confused mumbling.

The Innovation Paradox

You keep telling everyone you want their ideas, but somehow they're not forthcoming. People seem hesitant to speak up, and when you use all your skills to bring them out, they do – but their suggestions feel safe and uninspired. Meanwhile, your competitors seem to be bubbling with creativity.

The Middle Management Muddle

Your middle managers are caught in a perpetual squeeze. They're expected to be strategic with their superiors and operational with their teams. The result? They're excellent at neither, and everyone's frustrated.

The "Us vs Them" Divide

Despite your best efforts at creating "one team," there's an invisible wall between leadership and everyone else. You hear phrases like "them upstairs" or "the people at the top," even though you've tried to create an open-door policy.

The Resource Hoarding

Departments protect their budgets, headcount, and information like dragons guarding treasure. Cross-functional projects feel like diplomatic negotiations between suspicious nations.

The Engagement Enigma

Your employee engagement scores are mediocre at best, despite the table tennis table in the break room and the monthly pizza parties. People do their jobs, but the spark is missing.

How Did We Get Here?

To understand why we're stuck with this problematic model, we need to take a quick journey back in time.

Traditional hierarchy models have existed for thousands of years, from ancient dictatorships through to military structures, where the leaders were educated, wealthy, powerful, and well-connected. Ordinary people or soldiers on the other hand, were considered uneducated and disposable for the greater good.

Even some of the larger, established churches and faith organisations built structures based on this model. Their leaders were also educated (perhaps in Latin), wealthy, powerful, able to articulate well, and wielded massive influence. Parishioners were uneducated, unable to read or question for themselves, and so were informed only by those at the top – filtered through the ranks and whispers.

The roots of our current business structures can be traced back to the Industrial Revolution of the late 18th and 19th centuries. As factories began to replace small workshops and cottage industries, the need for an organisational structure emerged.

The pioneers of industrialisation, such as Richard Arkwright and Henry Ford, needed a way to coordinate the efforts of large numbers of workers, many of whom had little formal education or technical skill. The solution they landed on was the hierarchical, command-and-control model of the military.

In these models, decision-making power is concentrated at the top of the organisational pyramid. Orders and information flow downward through clear chains of leadership. People at the bottom of the hierarchy were expected to follow instructions – they were not expected to think independently or question those above them.

This approach worked successfully for many, many years. However, we are now in a new age – an age of information and education: the digital age. Organisations now have the opportunity to tap into the education and intelligence of everyone.

In this context, the old industrial hierarchies are not just outdated – they're actively counterproductive. When decision-making is bottlenecked at the top, organisations can't respond quickly to changing market conditions. When people are treated like interchangeable parts, they have little incentive to contribute their full talents and insights. They are independent thinkers, and some people may have higher IQs or sharper insights than their managers! If they are not led well, they become disenfranchised and eventually leave the organisation in search of something that keeps them engaged.

But guess what? We're not in the Industrial Revolution anymore. We are in the knowledge age.

I remember working on a military project many years ago that spelled this problem out plainly. It was a meeting in a large room with about 30 people from many engineering suppliers, gathered to help the military with an automotive project. It was part of a much bigger, high-profile contract valued at over £2 billion.

We met in this big room and waited for the acting Colonel to arrive, share the engineering challenge, and inspire the suppliers. The larger-than-life (and loud) Colonel marched into the room and attempted to motivate everyone in an 'instruct and command' style – as if all were expected to stand to attention when he spoke. In this meeting, he displayed no emotional intelligence at all.

As the project progressed over several months, many of the suppliers struggled. Their young, intelligent engineers found it uninspiring to work within this culture. They disengaged. They were not motivated by this hierarchy. They were motivated by making a meaningful contribution, being valued, and feeling a sense of belonging. This was denied to them because the structure and framework around the project were not effectively designed to allow contributions to flow in both directions.

They voted with their feet and left their jobs, causing massive disruption and cost to the project.

People react this way because humans fundamentally seek identity, worth, value, purpose, security, community, and love.

Many of today's successful organisations require something entirely different. They need to adapt rapidly to change, with innovation at every level, while engaging their employees' full thinking capacity and keeping them connected. They require fast, multidirectional communication, coupled with collaborative problem-solving approaches.

Yet, we are still using an organisational model designed for the cotton mill! We must adjust for today's workers – those who have knowledge and global awareness at their fingertips.

Above all, a different kind of leadership behaviour is needed.

KEY CONCEPT: OUTDATED HIERARCHY

Traditional hierarchies originated in the Industrial Revolution, when workers had little education and technical skill. Today, in an age of information and education, these outdated structures discourage organisations from tapping into the intelligence of everyone.

The Cost of Looking Down

The cost of this outdated framework and disengaged workforce is potentially staggering. According to Gallup's research, a disengaged employee costs an organisation at least 18% of their annual salary through increased absence, lower productivity, and therefore, reduced profitability. But the true price is even higher.

Financial Costs

Consider the opportunities lost to slow decision-making, or the mounting recruitment costs from constant employee turnover. Think about the resources wasted through poor communication channels, and the market opportunities missed because rigid structures couldn't respond in time.

Human Costs

The human toll is equally concerning. We see rising stress-related illness and burnout across organisations and mental struggles at an all-time high. Employees go through the motions, disengaged from their work. Talented people seek out more progressive environments, while leaders find themselves increasingly isolated and overwhelmed.

Strategic Costs

Strategically, the impact cuts even deeper. Organisations struggle to adapt quickly to market changes. Innovation happens despite the structure – not because of it. Meanwhile, competitors with more agile structures take the lead, making sustainable growth increasingly difficult. Sometimes, you may even wish you were a small, agile organisation again.

KEY CONCEPT: THE REAL COST OF DISENGAGEMENT

A disengaged employee costs an organisation at least 18% of their annual salary through increased absence and lower productivity. But the true price extends to missed opportunities, slow decision making, employee turnover, stress-related illness, and strategic stagnation. These aren't signs of poor performance – they're symptoms of a framework that has outlived its usefulness.

The Leader's Burden

As the leader, these challenges likely feel very personal. You might find yourself feeling responsible for everything yet in control of very little. Perhaps you struggle to get accurate information about what's really happening in your organisation. Many leaders miss the hands-on satisfaction of their previous roles, wondering why implementing change feels like pushing water uphill.

You're not alone. These aren't signs that you're a poor leader – they're symptoms of a framework that's outlived its usefulness.

In the next chapter, we'll explore what we can learn from nature's most successful organisational structure – the tree. But first, take a moment to reflect on your own experience. Consider which of these challenges resonate most strongly in your organisation. Calculate the financial potential cost this past year through disengagement and slow decision-making.

Think about how much energy you spend fighting against your current structure rather than working with it. Now, remember those olive trees I described at the beginning – their sturdy trunks supporting vibrant canopies of leaves dancing in the sunlight. Each leaf moving freely, yet perfectly connected to its source of strength. Each branch reaching naturally toward opportunity. The whole tree working in harmony.

Now imagine your organisation transformed like this. Picture your people as vibrant and engaged as those dancing leaves, each one energised and supported by the structure beneath them. Imagine resources, information, and insight flowing as naturally as sap through a healthy tree. See your organisation adapting and growing as smoothly as branches reaching for sunlight.

This isn't just a nice metaphor – it's a proven blueprint for organisational success. And in the chapters ahead, we'll discover exactly how to make this vision your reality.

2

Nature's Blueprint

In Plain Sight

L et me take you back to that London café, where I was
sitting with a client. You may recall he was sketching his
organisation chart in his notebook, and I was distracted
by the olive trees outside the window (my favourite tree).

Their sturdy trunks supported an explosion of branches reaching
skyward... an everyday model of growth.

A Tale of Two Growth Patterns

When we compare how organisations typically structure
themselves with how nature designs for growth, the contrast is striking.
The traditional Industrial Revolution model starts at the top, with
leadership forcing power and control downward while concentrating
resources at the peak. Growth becomes constrained by the very
structure meant to support it, with support awkwardly trying to flow
down against its natural tendency.

Nature, however, shows us a different way. A tree begins with
strong foundations, allowing energy to flow outward and upward
organically. Resources distribute themselves to where they're needed
most, and growth pushes into areas that are uncrowded. Most

importantly, support flows from the core, nourishing every part of the system.

The difference is fundamental to how organisations need to function and grow.

Learning from the Masters of Growth

Trees are nature's master class in organisational design. While humans have been experimenting with organisational structures, trees have been perfecting their growth systems. Their success offers us practical lessons.

Consider strength through support. A tree's trunk doesn't dominate or control its branches, instead, it dedicates its existence to supporting them. The trunk grows thicker and stronger not to assert greater authority, but to enable its branches to reach further and support more growth. As the organisation grows taller and more complex, the trunk's role in support becomes even more crucial.

Resource distribution in trees puts our best supply chain systems to shame. They've perfected a two-way flow that never clogs or breaks down. Water and nutrients surge upward through the trunk's transport system, while energy produced in the leaves flows back down. There's no hoarding of resources, no departmental stockpiling, no power plays with budgets. Everything moves where it's needed, when it's needed, in a continuous exchange that benefits the whole system.

Their approach to growth is remarkably different from our rigid business plans. Trees don't set unrealistic growth targets or try to force expansion in predetermined directions. Instead, they grow opportunistically yet systematically. They extend towards sunlight where it appears, send roots towards water when they sense it, and develop new branches where space allows. Each growth decision is both opportunistic and systematic.

 ## KEY CONCEPT: NATURE'S GROWTH MODEL

While traditional organisations push control downward from the top, nature shows us a different way. A tree begins with strong foundations, allowing energy to flow outward and upward organically. Resources distribute themselves to where they're needed most, and growth pushes into areas that are uncrowded. Most importantly, support flows from the core, nourishing every part of the system.

But perhaps most revolutionary is how trees demonstrate true hierarchy. In a tree, every part has its distinct role and purpose, but none is treated as lesser than another. The leaves, which we might consider analogous to front-line workers in traditional organisational charts, are not at the bottom of the structure as stated earlier, they are the crown of the whole operation.

They're the primary value creators, turning sunlight into energy that feeds the entire system. Without healthy, thriving leaves, the most impressive trunk and branches become nothing more than an elaborate frame.

When we start seeing our organisations through this lens – as living, breathing organic systems rather than static mechanical structures, everything changes. This shift in perspective isn't just about moving boxes around on an organisation chart. It's about fundamentally rethinking how we view organisational health, growth, and success.

Your organisation is a living system, not a static mechanical structure.

From Theory to Practice

Let's return to the CEO, Jade, and her structure. The key elements of her organisation take on new meaning when viewed through nature's lens.

The root system forms her external support structures – her key external relationships provide her with foundational stability. Her own leadership role transforms into the trunk, providing core strength shaped by her experience and values. She facilitates, offers protection and focusses on her skills to be an enabler to growth.

Her leadership teams become the branches, extending the organisation's reach into spaces. They provide flexibility and support new growth wherever opportunity arises. Finally, at the crown, value creation happens through the leaves. Customer interaction, product innovation, and customer insight provide clear indications of organisational health and generate profit for the whole living system to exist and thrive.

KEY CONCEPT: CROWN VALUE CREATORS

In a tree, the leaves are not at the bottom of the structure — they are the crown of the whole operation. They're the primary value creators, turning sunlight into energy that feeds the entire system. Without healthy, thriving leaves, the most impressive trunk and branches become nothing more than an elaborate frame. This should invert our traditional thinking about organisational hierarchy and transform how we view the roles of front-line workers.

Looking Forward

Remember, every mighty oak started as a small acorn that grew according to nature's process. Your organisation can do the same. In the next chapter, we'll explore each element of a natural tree, including the roots – those often-forgotten support systems that keep everything stable and nourished.

For now, though, just let this idea take root ;-) What if the most natural way to grow your organisation was also the most sustainable?

3

Dendrology (The Study of Trees)

Understanding a Tree's System

Before we map our organisational roles onto nature's blueprint, let's understand the incredible design we're working with.

Take a moment to look at a tree – any tree. What do you notice first? Perhaps its overall shape, its height, or how its branches spread. However, there's so much more going on than meets the eye.

Whether it's a towering sycamore or a young sapling, they all share the same basic elements. Each of these elements has evolved to play a vital role in the tree's success. When we understand these elements and how they work together, we can start to see how we can transform our organisations.

So bear with me.

The Hidden Wonders Beneath Our Trees

Think about the biggest tree you've ever seen. Perhaps it was an ancient oak in a park, or a towering pine in a forest. Now imagine that same tree flipped upside down. Underneath that tree is another half that we never see, spreading just as wide and sometimes even deeper than the tree is tall.

Tree roots are nature's great hidden secret. While we can easily see how a tree grows above ground – its strong trunk, spreading branches, and dancing leaves – something equally amazing is happening in the soil beneath our feet.

These roots aren't just simple anchors holding the tree in place (although they do that job brilliantly). They're more like an underground treasure-hunting network. Main roots spread out from the trunk like spokes on a bicycle wheel. From these big roots, smaller roots branch off, getting thinner and thinner until they're finer than a strand of hair.

KEY CONCEPT: THE HIDDEN FOUNDATION

Beneath every magnificent tree lies an equally impressive root system that we never see. These roots aren't just invisible anchors – they're sophisticated networks that selectively gather resources, communicate with other trees through the "Wood Wide Web", store energy for challenging times, and continuously adapt.

Your organisation's hidden support systems are equally vital to its survival and growth.

Some trees send one massive root straight down, like a giant carrot, searching for water deep underground. Others spread their roots wide but shallow, like an enormous upside-down umbrella just under the soil. Most trees actually do both, adapting to whatever works best for where they are growing.

But here's the truly wonderful part: at the very tips of the tiniest roots are root hairs – thousands of them – too small to see without a microscope. These tiny root hairs are like the tree's fingers, carefully selecting what the tree needs from the soil. They don't just soak up everything they find, they choose exactly what the tree requires for it to grow strong and healthy.

Even more amazing is how roots talk to each other. Yes, you read that right, trees actually communicate underground! They connect with each other through tiny threads of friendly fungi in the soil, creating what scientists call the *"Wood Wide Web."* Through these fungal connections, trees share food and even warn each other about dangers, like harmful insects.

Roots are also like your kitchen freezer, storing food for when it's needed. During summer, when there's plenty of sunlight and water, roots stock up on energy and nutrients. Then, in winter, or when times are tough, the tree can use these stored supplies to stay healthy.

And they never stop exploring. Unlike the sturdy, stable trunk above ground, roots are always growing and changing. They grow towards water, work their way around rocks, and multiply wherever they find good soil. If they discover a particularly rich patch of earth, they'll send out extra root hairs to gather all the goodness they can find.

In the world of trees, what happens underground is just as important as what we can see reaching for the sky.

The Tree's Tower of Strength

When you look at a tree trunk, you can see remarkable stories. Some are straight and true, aiming directly at the sky. Others twist and turn, bearing the marks of decades of growth, challenge, and survival. Each trunk is unique, like a book sharing its life story through its bark, knots, and patterns.

But what's really going on inside this living tower? Cut through any trunk and you'll find a masterpiece of natural engineering, built up in layers over years of growth.

At the very centre lies the *heartwood*. Despite being the oldest part of the trunk, it's actually dead tissue, however, that doesn't mean it's not important. As the tree grows, it fills these central cells with special compounds that make them incredibly strong. The heartwood is like the tree's backbone, providing the strength to hold up tons of branches, leaves, and sometimes even snow.

Surrounding the heartwood is the living part of the trunk – the *sapwood*. This layer is the tree's transport system, moving water and nutrients up from the roots to the highest leaves. It works rather like a bundle of drinking straws, with special cells forming tubes that carry this precious cargo upward. At the same time, different tubes carry food produced in the leaves back down to feed the rest of the tree.

Just outside the sapwood is one of the most remarkable parts of the trunk – the *cambium layer*. This thin sheet of cells is where all the trunk's growth happens. Each year, it adds new layers of wood on the inside and new bark on the outside, making the trunk thicker and stronger. These layers form the tree rings we can see in cut stumps, each one marking a year in the tree's life.

Finally, on the outside is the *bark* – but it's far more than just a wrapping. Bark is the tree's protection system, defending against insects, diseases, animal damage, and extreme weather. Some trees, like the mighty redwoods, grow bark so thick it can even protect them from forest fires.

As the trunk grows taller and thicker, it often develops character marks – knots where branches once grew, twisted grain patterns from adapting to strong winds, or scars where it healed from injury. These aren't flaws, they're signs of the tree's resilience and history, telling the world how it adapted and grew stronger through challenges.

Just like human skin can heal after a scratch, a tree's trunk can repair itself when damaged. It grows special tissue around wounds, gradually covering them over time. Some old trees bear the marks of events that happened hundreds of years ago.

What's truly amazing is how all these parts work together. The trunk must be strong enough to support enormous weight, flexible enough to sway in winds without breaking, and still keep its vital transport systems working smoothly. It must grow both taller and thicker while maintaining its strength, and protect itself while still being able to breathe through tiny pores in the bark.

The trunk is a living tower that grows stronger every year while continuing to nourish and protect the entire tree.

The Art of Branching Out

When you look up through a tree's canopy, you will see an incredible natural pattern. Each tree species has its own signature way of branching – oaks spread wide and strong, poplars reach straight up, and olive trees twist and turn in wonderfully dramatic ways.

But there's clever design behind this beautiful display. Tree branches are masterpieces of natural engineering, solving a complex puzzle: how to spread out to catch maximum sunlight while staying strong enough to support their own weight, handle strong winds, and carry the burden of leaves, flowers, and fruit.

The way branches grow is fascinating. Each major branch starts at the trunk as a tiny bud. As it grows, it creates a special joint with the trunk, a complex pattern of interwoven wood fibres that creates incredible strength.

Branches work in layers of responsibility. The primary branches – those big limbs coming straight from the trunk are like the tree's arms. They create the tree's basic shape and support everything that grows from them. You'll often see trees with just three or four of these major branches. This isn't random, it's the perfect number to create a stable, well-balanced crown without overcrowding.

From these main branches grow the secondary branches, spreading out to fill the available space. They're more flexible than the main branches and can bend with wind or under the weight of snow. They're also opportunists – they'll grow towards any patch of sunlight they can find, twisting and turning to reach the light.

Watch how branches share space. They rarely cross or tangle. Instead, they spread out to give each other room. When branches do touch, they often develop thicker bark at that point to protect themselves from rubbing damage. It's like they've worked out a careful peace treaty about personal space.

Perhaps most remarkable is how branches adapt to their conditions. A tree growing in an open field will spread its branches wide and low. The same species growing in a forest will send its branches upward, racing its neighbours for sunlight. If you cut back a branch, nearby branches will gradually adjust their growth to fill the gap.

Each branch is also a self-contained transport system. Like the trunk, inside every branch runs a complex network of tubes carrying water and nutrients up to the leaves, and bringing the food created by the leaves back down. The branch must keep these vital supply lines working while bending in the wind and supporting its load.

In winter, when trees lose their leaves, the true artistry of branches becomes visible. That's when you can really see the natural architecture

– how each branch divides into smaller branches at just the right angles for strength and balance. It's like looking at the tree's blueprint.

Every fork, every twist, every spread of branches tells the story of that tree's journey towards the light.

The Crowning Glory – A Tree's Living Energy Makers

Have you ever really looked at a leaf? Each one is an incredibly efficient natural factory, transforming sunlight, water, and air into food for the entire tree. But that's just the beginning of their remarkable story.

Leaves are the tree's crown, and like any crown, they make a statement. A tree's leaves tell us if it's thriving or struggling, if it's getting enough water, if it's fighting off disease, or if it's stressed by its environment. They're nature's most visible health indicators.

The way leaves arrange themselves is a marvel of natural efficiency. Look up through a tree's canopy and you'll see very few leaves directly above others. Instead, they position themselves like tiles on a roof, each catching sunlight without shading those below. Some trees' leaves will even twist their stems to move into better positions. This isn't random, it's a carefully choreographed dance to catch every possible ray of sunlight.

Each leaf is also a masterpiece of engineering. The surface of a leaf is covered in a waxy coating that protects it while letting in light. Underneath are layers of cells arranged like solar panels, ready to capture sunlight's energy. The underside is dotted with tiny pores that can open and close, controlling how much water vapour escapes and how much carbon dioxide enters – a ventilation system more sophisticated than most office buildings.

But leaves don't just make food – they're also the tree's cooling system. On hot days, they release water vapour through those tiny pores, creating a cooling effect just like human sweating. A large tree can pump hundreds of litres of water from soil to air on a summer's day, helping to cool its immediate environment.

Leaves are also remarkably adaptable. Trees growing in full sun often have smaller, thicker leaves to prevent water loss, while those in shade develop larger, thinner leaves to catch more light. Some leaves toughen up in response to insects trying to eat them, while others can change their chemistry to become less tasty to predators.

As the seasons change, leaves put on one of nature's most spectacular shows. The green chlorophyll that powers their food factories breaks down, revealing the yellow and orange pigments that were there all along.

Even when leaves fall, they continue to serve the tree. Decomposing leaves create a rich layer of nutrients in the soil, feeding the very roots that will supply next year's new leaves. It's nature's perfect recycling system.

The relationship between a tree's leaves and the rest of its structure is the essence of cooperation. The leaves need the trunk and branches to lift them into the sunlight and to supply them with water. In return, they send energy-rich food back down to support the entire tree. Neither could survive without the other.

When you see leaves dancing in the breeze, remember you're watching the visible part of an incredible partnership.

Growth Patterns

Nature's approach to growth challenges our conventional thinking. While we often expect growth to be steady and predictable, trees show us a different pattern.

Even when nothing appears to be happening on the surface, trees are busy with hidden preparation. During winter, while branches stand bare, chemical changes are taking place inside, root systems are developing, and energy reserves are being carefully managed. When the right conditions arrive – perhaps a warm spring day or a gap in the canopy – this preparation enables dramatic growth that seems to appear overnight.

Trees also show great flexibility in their growth strategy. During challenging conditions, they might focus on strengthening roots rather than extending branches. What's fascinating is how they grow in response to stress – the wind that threatens to force a tree over actually stimulates growth that makes it stronger.

KEY CONCEPT: PURPOSEFUL GROWTH

Trees don't grow randomly – they grow with purpose. During challenging conditions, they might focus on strengthening roots rather than extending branches. Even mature trees continue to develop, focusing on complex structures or strengthening their core. True growth isn't just about size, it's about developing exactly what's needed, when it's needed.

Age doesn't stop growth either, it just changes its nature. While young trees focus on reaching upward, mature trees often concentrate on developing more complex structures or strengthening their core. Throughout all stages, every bit of growth serves a purpose whether reaching toward light, strengthening support, or extending roots.

In this way, trees demonstrate that true growth isn't just about size, it's about developing exactly what's needed, when it's needed, due to its ever-changing environment. This is how they survive in the long term.

Looking Forward

You made it! Throughout this chapter, we've explored nature's proven design. At first glance, you might ask why a leader should care about tree biology. If you are wanting to build something strong, sustainable, and capable of constant growth, then look at what nature has already mastered.

As we move forward, we'll see how this understanding transforms organisational leadership. Every element we've explored offers practical solutions to the real challenges you may face daily. The wisdom is there, tested by time, proven by survival.

Let's now discover how to put it to work in your organisation.

4

Your Hidden Foundation – The Root System

The Forgotten Foundation

When was the last time you saw crucial suppliers and services on an organisational chart? I never have. Roots are the critical element of a growing structure. The same is true for your organisation – those invisible support structures are absolutely vital to your survival and growth.

Let's start applying the tree metaphor to your organisation and its roles, beginning with your roots.

Nature's Support Network

Remember what you read about roots in the previous chapter? In nature, roots serve multiple critical functions. They anchor the tree firmly to the ground, gather water and nutrients from the soil, store energy for future growth, and even communicate with other trees through underground networks.

Your organisation's support systems serve similarly vital roles. Let's look at the principal ones.

Financial Roots

Just as a tree's roots selectively absorb exactly what nutrients it needs, your banking relationships, investment partners, and financial advisors create channels for resources to flow. Like a tree's water-gathering roots, they ensure your organisation has what it needs to thrive. Insurance providers add crucial protection, allowing confident growth even in uncertain conditions.

- Banking relationships
- Investment partners
- Financial advisors
- Accountants
- Credit facilities
- Insurance providers

Legal Roots

Like a tree's protective root barriers that prevent harmful substances from entering, your corporate lawyers, employment specialists, and regulatory advisors provide your protective framework. Intellectual property protection preserves what makes your organisation unique. These roots keep you safe.

- Corporate lawyers

- Employment law specialists

- Intellectual property advisors

- Regulatory compliance experts

- Industry bodies

- Standards organisations

Knowledge Roots

Similar to the way tree roots share information through underground fungal networks, your industry networks, research partnerships, and advisory boards broaden your learning and innovation. Professional associations and training providers ensure continuous development. These connections help your organisation grow smarter and more adaptable.

- Industry networks

- Research partnerships

- Academic connections

- Training providers

- Mentors and coaches

- Advisory boards

- Professional associations

Governance Roots

Just as anchor roots provide stability while allowing a tree to grow and flex in strong winds, your shareholders, trustees, boards, and committees provide strategic guidance and oversight. Together with governance professionals, they ensure your organisation grows sustainably and ethically.

- Shareholders

- Board of Trustees

- External Directors

- Advisory Board

- Regulatory Bodies

- Board of Directors

- Audit Committee

- Risk Committee

- Ethics Committee

- Governance Committee

- Remuneration Committee

Community Roots

Like the way tree roots interweave with their entire ecosystem, your local government relationships, community partnerships, and supplier networks connect you to your broader community. Environmental and social connections help your organisation and its people flourish outside of its core.

- Local government relationships

- Community partnerships

- Supplier networks

- Industry associations

- Chamber of Commerce

- Environmental groups

- Charitable connections

Nurturing Your Roots

These foundation systems require regular nurturing. The stronger and healthier your root systems, the more your organisation can grow and thrive in the future.

KEY CONCEPT: FIVE VITAL ROOT SYSTEMS

Just as a tree's roots provide stability and nourishment, your organisation depends on five critical support systems:

- *Financial roots provide resources and protection.*

- *Legal roots create protective frameworks.*

- *Knowledge roots facilitate learning and innovation.*

- *Governance roots ensure sustainable growth.*

- *Community roots connect you to your broader ecosystem.*

How deep do your relationships go? How widespread is your support network? Where might you be vulnerable? Just as a tree needs different types of roots – some deep, some widespread – your organisation needs various types of support.

Next, consider where you need to grow new roots. Perhaps you've identified gaps in your support network, or maybe you're planning expansion into new areas. Remember, you can't just throw money at root development – these are based on relationships and need time and genuine engagement to flourish. Do you send them your newsletters? Do you invite them to company events? Do they feel invested in your organisation?

Don't wait for the storm to test your root strength (remember the recent global pandemic!). Regular attention to your support systems helps prevent problems before they arise.

The Foundation Is Set

As we've explored these different root systems, it becomes clear that modern organisations are far more complex than a simple organisational chart suggests. These hidden foundations – financial, legal, knowledge, governance, and community relationships, are as vital to your success as roots are to a tree.

And this brings us to a crucial transition point. All of these support systems converge at one place – the base of the trunk. In our next chapter, we'll explore your role as the principal leader through an entirely new lens. We'll discover how understanding the trunk's three elements – heartwood, transport system, and protective bark, offers a revolutionary perspective on leadership that's perfectly suited to today's business environment.

KEY CONCEPT: RELATIONSHIP NURTURING

Root systems require regular attention and genuine relationship-building — not just transactional exchanges. How deep do your support relationships go? How widespread is your network? Don't wait for challenges to test your root strength; regular attention to these foundational systems prevents problems before they arise.

5

Leadership's True Role – The Trunk

Strength at the Core

Remember when I was having coffee with my client in London, admiring the olive trees outside the café window? They had a unique, gnarly trunk, bearing the marks of decades of growth, challenge, and adaptation. These weren't the perfectly straight, unblemished trunks you might see in a plant nursery. They were character-filled columns of strength and resilience, each telling its own graphic story of survival and growth.

As my client discussed his leadership challenges, his stories of success, his failures, struggles, and overcoming, I couldn't help but notice how the tree's trunk mirrored his storytelling. It too was full of scars, wounds, marks of being stretched and growing, and here it stood

— the central support to this beautiful tree. Not succeeding despite its battles, but as a result of them.

Nature's Leadership Model

In a tree, the trunk isn't the boss — it's the servant. Its entire purpose is to support and enable growth above while staying connected to the nourishing roots below. This is perhaps nature's most profound lesson for leaders: Leadership isn't about being at the top like a shining star; it's about being at the core, providing the strength, resources, and support that enables others to grow. That is a mindset shift right there. Some people understand that easily, while others less so, because it's such an inverted way of thinking compared to what many assume.

I remember one client who had reached a ceiling in a manufacturing business. He was from a Middle Eastern background, and his work culture was to work hard for success. To do really well meant working even harder and more hours. It took some time, but when he got his thinking around the concept that he could achieve more by empowering others to grow their element of the business, the ceiling was lifted. Today, it's a very large and successful organisation.

KEY CONCEPT: LEADERSHIP AS SUPPORT

In a tree, the trunk isn't the boss — it's the servant. This represents a fundamental mindset shift: Leadership isn't about being at the top; it's about being at the core, providing the strength, resources, and support that enables others to grow.

The Three Elements of Leadership

Just as a tree's trunk has three distinct layers – heartwood, transport system, and bark – effective leadership comprises three essential elements. Let's explore each one.

1: The Heartwood: Your Core Strength

At the centre of every trunk lies the heartwood. It's the oldest, strongest part of the tree, providing the structural integrity that keeps everything stable. In your organisation, this represents your core values, vision, and culture, and it requires stability. If this already exists and you have joined the organisation after these have been established, then you better share the same ones, or find a different organisation. It is hard to fake for very long! Therefore, to sustain that stability you need to be completely authentic. Well-known books talk about the 'why' – tapping into the true, authentic values of a person. This is the only way you can sustain the relentless requirement of providing consistent core strength to your organisation, day after day.

Your heartwood must have clarity and demonstrate consistency in values, maintain strong principles, and remain solid during storms. This means you need to know yourself well – what are you strong at? What scares you? What do you shy away from? Without these qualities being solid and visible, the entire structure becomes vulnerable to someone else's values.

I have witnessed many leaders taking years to understand what is at the core of their being. They start by thinking it's A, and when nothing really changes, they conclude that A wasn't authentic to them.

They try B, and similarly, nothing really changes. Then they dig deep and discover C. C is authentic, and that becomes their heartwood.

Even simple things like dreams and ambitions can be revealing. I once coached a gentleman who was adamant that his ambition and dream was around owning a particular Maserati high performance car. I arranged a test drive for him, and the test car happened to be the model and the exact colour he dreamt of. He drove it, loved it, and concluded that it wasn't what his dreams were made of after all.

Everyone is on a journey that is unique to them, and that is OK. My point is, make sure your heartwood is fully aligned with the requirements of the organisation, or you will struggle; the trunk will be weak.

2: The Transport System: Flow and Connection

Surrounding the heartwood is the transport system – layers of tissue that move water and nutrients up and down the tree. In your organisation, this represents how resources, information, challenges, and support flow through the structure.

Much of this requires you to be the Chief Storyteller. You are the connector between your network of people who make up your roots and your key limbs – the primary branches. So many CEOs I've worked with rely on telepathy! They just expect people to know what they are thinking or what their priorities are. You must create clear channels for communication flowing both up and down the organisation. This includes ensuring timely and appropriate resource distribution, facilitating knowledge sharing, delivering both challenge and support where needed, and maintaining open feedback loops throughout the structure above and below ground.

Many organisations suffer from blocked transport systems – information doesn't flow, resources get stuck, feedback dies in middle management. Like a tree with blocked vessels, the organisation starts to show signs of stress.

I see this a lot in semi-successful organisations. The leader is strong, bullish, driven, results-oriented. They are also unapproachable, have little time, patience, or inclination to develop their teams. This results in them becoming a single point of original thought, information and energy. Their transport system is one-way! They will have disengaged people all around them.

What are some of the reasons that resources do not flow in your organisation?

Ignorance over affordability

If an organisation does not know its commercials in specific numbers (the language of business), it cannot make informed decisions about spending and investment. It simply doesn't know if it's wise to invest in X or Y, and because it doesn't know, the answer will generally be a no to spending, no to resources, and no flow. This could be as basic as cash flow and projections of income and outgoings.

Lack of courage over difficult conversations

If you know you will get a hard time convincing others about the wisdom of a particular investment in staff, training, resources, or whatever, you may be tempted to put your head in the sand. You will not invest because it will avoid the difficult conversation. This can be more common when you are time-challenged because you do not have the time to explain. It's also very short-term and lacks courage and conviction.

Adjustable Binoculars

A good leader has the ability to adjust their focus from short distance to long range. A great leader can do this at any time – short, long, mid, long, short, etc.

Have you ever stared at a stereogram? Stereograms are pictures that look like random patterns on a page, but people who can do them will suddenly see something with great clarity. This happens ONLY when you look at the picture right in front of you but focus into the distance. Initially, the picture is blurred, but as you focus at the correct long distance, suddenly you get perfect clarity! You may be the only one who can see it clearly.

These leaders can see what the needs are right now. They can see what will happen if they do or don't make a decision. They can see the cost of not making a decision. They can see the short-term pain for the long-term gain, or vice versa. If you lack this skill, you may be restricting the two-way flow from within your organisation.

What is preventing you from focusing past the obvious and into the distance?

Awareness is sometimes curative, so recognising that this could be you is the first major step. Invert your thinking to that of enabling, developing, teaching, nurturing, equipping, and releasing the minds and skills of your key people. This will transform and multiply your people's results. Then ensure they do the same for their direct reports.

Emotional Intelligence

It has been the focus of much research in recent years to discover that great leaders are highly Emotionally Intelligent (EQ). You didn't necessarily need a high EQ to operate in the historical organisational structure, barking down from the top, or as a Colonel in the military. However, in today's world, barking commands does not necessarily get things done well. Instead, the ability to inspire, motivate, and communicate well are the keys. These skills are wrapped around EQ. This is your ability to know yourself well and to have a good grasp of understanding those around you. And whilst you may be surrounded by people with high IQ (which can diminish with age), EQ continues to grow – which is good to know!

I love the work of Dr Martyn L. Newman in developing Emotional Capital Reports – quantitative reports that help you recognise, improve, and build emotional skills. I have worked with Martyn for many years and helped many leaders using his tools. These will not only improve you as a leader, but all-round in life with friends and family relationships too. Understand when your straightforwardness, optimism, self-assurance, and self-reliance are helpful. Build your skills in empathy (not sympathy), relationship skills, and self-confidence.

Take an EQ test. Make sure you know your blind spots and develop them.

3: The Protective Bark: Wisdom and Resilience

The outer layer of a trunk isn't just packaging, it's a sophisticated protection system.

Bark is formed through previous growth and subsequent stretching. This creates a protective barrier. A leader's previous growth and experience that stretched them, even broke them, gives them a unique, gnarly quality that can be used to protect the organisation. They provide wisdom. A leader who has experienced the ups and downs of leading through the global pandemic, for example, now has a toughened quality to cope in difficult environments. A leader who has gone out of business before or had family catastrophes to deal with may now well know some telltale signs of incoming danger to the organisation and can steer and adjust accordingly.

Experience, both good and bad, is still helpful experience as you face making wise choices.

I believe wisdom is an essential trait of leadership today. Oh, I wish some governmental leaders created policies and decisions with more wisdom!

Your gnarly, knotty, rough exterior – your bark – can protect and safeguard you, your organisation, and others around you.

As the principal leader, you also have the responsibility to create time in your schedule to make sure your organisation is safe from foreign bodies attacking it. For example, is it legally compliant? Is it secure? Are there any environmental, political, or social changes coming that could affect the health of your organisation?

Growing

A tree's trunk grows in two ways – it gets taller, and it gets thicker. Your leadership should develop similarly:

Growing taller represents reaching new heights in your own improvement as your organisation requires new growth, perhaps through expansion, influence, market presence, etc. Invest in your own training, your skills, hire a coach who can see what you cannot, become better than you are today.

Growing thicker represents strength through accumulating further experience, growing in wisdom, and building wider relationships.

KEY CONCEPT: THE THREE ELEMENTS OF LEADERSHIP

Effective leadership comprises three essential elements, mirroring a tree's trunk: Heartwood (your authentic core values and vision), Transport System (how resources, information, and communication flow), and Bark (the protective wisdom gained through experience). All three must be developed for the organisation to thrive.

The Marks of Growth

The knots, scars, and twisted grain patterns tell a story of challenge and adaptation. Your leadership journey will leave similar marks – not blemishes to be hidden, but evidence of your learning and growth. Wear them with pride.

Every challenge you face has the potential to strengthen your core, improve your systems, enhance your protection, and add to your wisdom. These experiences become part of your leadership growth. You are unique, your experience is unique, and your values and culture are unique. Allow your living organisation to grow because of them, not in spite of them.

Remember: everything above you, the 'trunk', depends on your support. The stronger and more effective your leadership core, the more your organisation can grow. But that strength isn't about rigidity, like a glass column – it's about providing stable and flexible support.

Looking Forward

As you reflect on your leadership role, consider the state of your core elements. Examine the strength of your heartwood, assess how well your transport systems flow, and evaluate the effectiveness of your protective layer. Think about where you might need to develop in order to enable others better.

In our next chapter, we'll explore how your primary branches – your key people, divisions, and departments – grow from this central support, and how they, in turn, support further growth.

Remember: the mightiest trees don't have the prettiest trunks – they have the strongest ones. Your role isn't to look perfect; it's to provide the solid, reliable support your organisation needs to thrive, day after day.

6

Your Key Growth Routes – Primary Branches

Nature's First Extension

Have you noticed how trees often have just three or four major branches extending from their trunk? Consider those olive trees I keep talking about. Farmers have learned, over thousands of years, to cultivate them with only a few primary branches to maximise fruit production. This isn't by accident – it's to ensure each branch gets more sunlight and resources to thrive, by giving them the freedom to have space and grow in the sun.

KEY CONCEPT: STRATEGIC DIVISION

Too many primary branches can weaken the entire structure. The quality and strength of these few key divisions or leadership roles determine your organisation's future growth potential.

This insight holds a vital lesson for organisations: not every function needs to report directly to the leader. In fact, too many primary branches can weaken the whole structure. The question then becomes: what should these primary branches look like in your organisation?

Just as a tree's primary branches form its fundamental structure and shape, your key divisions and leadership roles form the essential framework of your organisation...

The Power of Primary Branches

In your organisation, primary branches represent your major divisions or key leadership roles – perhaps Operations, Finance, Sales, or Product Development. Like tree branches, each needs to be strong enough to support its own network of smaller branches and leaves.

I worked with a marketing agency that had everyone reporting to Chris, the CEO. Everyone had access and influence. He was fairly progressive and uncomfortable with the Victorian top-down structure he inherited, so the only other structure he knew was a flat one – everyone reporting to him. The result? Everyone's focus was like a small boat in a storm, changing direction every week. When he reorganised into fewer primary reports, with clear responsibilities, everything began to work better, and the direction of travel was more deliberate and effective. Supporting rather than directing people was initially a struggle for Chris. His value, he thought, was in the doing and directing (telling). Enabling people initially didn't feel like he had worked hard at the end of the day (he still liked to be the technician), but the satisfaction he eventually had in seeing his reports succeed was such a thrill for him. Now growth was possible.

Strong Joints

Primary branches need specific characteristics to function effectively. Remember the joint between the trunk and the primary branches in the 'Dendrology' chapter? It starts with a bud and a unique bond is formed in the fibres of the wood. The joint between the trunk and the primary branch is crucial – it's where strength flows from one to the other. In your organisation, this represents the relationship between the principal leader (the trunk) and the division heads (the primary limbs). This connection must be strong enough to handle stress, yet flexible enough to allow movement. It needs to be clear enough for resources to flow freely and trusted enough to maintain open communication and collaboration.

KEY CONCEPT: STRONG CONNECTIONS

The joint between the trunk and the primary branch is crucial – it's where strength flows from one to the other. In your organisation, this represents the relationship between the principal leader and the division heads. This connection must be strong enough to handle stress, yet flexible enough to allow movement.

Each primary branch must grow in its own direction, yet remain part of the whole system. Your key divisions need this same balance – a clear directional purpose combined with independent decision-making that allows expansion and growth as required, while contributing to the shared organisational vision and purpose.

How strong and trusted are your relationships with your primary branches? Are they the right people?

Supporting Secondary Growth

Primary branches aren't end points in themselves – they're launching pads for growth. Each should be capable of supporting its own network of secondary branches and leaves. They are like mini trunks, but without the additional network of roots.

I have seen CEOs employ and let go of quite a few people in those primary positions until they find the ones they can trust and invest emotionally in.

Train Them

Many of these management positions will have people managing in a way they think is appropriate. They may have had bad experiences of being managed in the past, so they manage in an opposite way. They may think that, based on the traditional chart designed for an uneducated workforce, they should be lording it over their people, directing and barking at them. After all, they are the ones who carry all the responsibility, right? They manage with a learned behaviour. Their actions are based on their experience and belief systems.

Train them in your wisdom. Do they hold strong relationships with their branches? Can their departments run well when they are not around? Do they communicate well in both directions? Do they know their numbers and, therefore, are able to make informed decisions when distributing the tree's resources? Can they zoom in and out? Are they strong in their core? Do they enable? Do they feel empowered to grow and take opportunities? They may well have these great traits already, but if not, train them, coach them.

Looking Forward

As you reflect on your primary branches – those key leaders and divisions in your organisation – consider not just their current state, but their potential. As a tree's major limbs, they should be both strong and flexible, capable of supporting growth while adapting to new opportunities.

The relationship you build with these primary branches will largely determine your organisation's future. They are your partners in growth, like your own limbs, they are your multipliers. Their strength becomes your organisation's strength; their growth enables your organisation's expansion.

In our next chapter, we'll explore how these primary branches nurture their own networks of teams and departments – the secondary growth that creates your organisation's full potential. But for now, remember: just as a tree doesn't need countless major branches to flourish, your organisation doesn't need layers of direct reports to thrive. What it needs is primary branches strongly connected, well-supported, and given the room to grow.

The quality of these connections and the space you give them to develop will determine whether your organisation merely functions or truly flourishes.

7

Where Growth Multiplies – Secondary Branches

The Power of Multiplication

L ook closely at any healthy tree and you'll notice that each primary branch doesn't just grow longer and longer – it divides and multiplies, creating an ever more intricate network of smaller branches.

This growth isn't random; it's strategic – nature's way of maximising opportunity by reaching into every available space for the greatest chance to develop.

In your organisation, secondary branches represent your sub-departments, specialist teams, and project groups. They're where your primary divisions subdivide to create more focused, specialised units. This is where your organisation's real complexity and capability grow.

The Natural Pattern

Nature follows certain rules when creating secondary branches. Each new branch must have sufficient space to grow. It is always responding to opportunity, much like branches reaching toward sunlight, and it requires strong and healthy support as its own foundation.

Secondary branches create the growth network. Each new branch provides opportunities for further growth, creating an exponential increase in your organisation's reach and capability.

KEY CONCEPT: MULTIPLICATION THROUGH SPECIALISATION

Secondary branches (departments, specialist teams, project groups) create your organisation's complexity and capability. Like a tree's branching network, each new specialised unit creates opportunities for further growth, leading to an exponential increase in reach and capability when given sufficient space and support.

Consider how this works in practice: a sales team might develop a specific expertise, which creates opportunities for specialist product development. This creates new service offerings, leading to new customer relationships, which in turn opens further growth possibilities.

Supporting Healthy Growth

How do you support this multiplication of capability while maintaining organisational health?

Every secondary branch needs clear responsibilities, defined territories, distinct purposes, and room for innovation. These branches must maintain strong connections to their primary branch through clear reporting lines, regular communication, resource sharing, and a strong shared purpose.

Identity Crisis

Many of the people in these management/supervisor roles would, at some point, have been promoted from being on the front line. This transition is often a crisis point for many. The identity shift from 'technician' to 'manager' often brings other baggage. From having one set of peers and friends, they suddenly find themselves with a completely different circle of colleagues who may not be immediately supportive.

This transition raises concerns about what happens to their previous workplace friendships and relationships. So, doubts start to creep in about their value in this role, and the reason they may have been promoted. Self-doubt appears, and overcompensation in behaviour can play out. When this new role is viewed, as per our tree model, as supporting and enabling someone, this shift is a lot easier to make.

KEY CONCEPT: THE IDENTITY TRANSITION

The shift from 'technician' to 'manager' brings challenges: new peer relationships, self-doubt about personal value, and uncertainty about previous friendships. When this new role is framed as supporting and enabling your team rather than controlling, this transition becomes significantly easier.

Nurturing Development

Just as a tree shows signs when its branches aren't healthy, your organisation will display symptoms when secondary structures are struggling. Watch for resource conflicts, unclear boundaries, communication tangles, inefficient duplication, cultural disconnection, and of course, disengaged people.

Supporting secondary growth requires a different approach from managing primary branches. It demands more local autonomy, faster decision-making, closer market connection, and greater flexibility. There is a difference between training a mature branch and nurturing new growth – both need support, but in different ways.

Looking Forward

Secondary growth multiplies your organisation's capabilities. Each new department or specialist team increases your reach, provided they have space to develop and a clear purpose.

The success we see at this level comes from balancing autonomy with connection. These teams need the freedom to respond to opportunities while maintaining strong bonds with their primary divisions.

Next, we'll turn to your organisation's value creators – the teams who create your product or interact directly with your customers and market. Like leaves in the sun, they're positioned to transform opportunity into growth.

Nature's wisdom is simple: structure serves purpose. Everything we've explored about branches – both primary and secondary – exists to support those who create value for your organisation.

8

Where Value Creation Happens - The Crown

The Visible Truth

When people look at a tree, what do they see first? Not the roots, and generally not the trunk or branches (unless it's winter). They see the leaves. The crown of the tree is what catches the eye and tells the world whether that tree is thriving or struggling, growing or dying.

Your organisation works the same way. Your front-line teams — the people who interact with customers, create products, deliver services — are the visible face of your organisation. They are not the bottom of anything; they are the crown of your organisation.

KEY CONCEPT: FRONT-LINE VALUE CREATORS

Your front-line teams are the crown of your organisation. Like leaves that transform sunlight into energy for the entire tree, these people create the value that sustains your entire organisation.

The tree metaphor for organisational structure is perfectly suited to the digital age, where workers are more connected, empowered, and knowledge-rich than ever before.

In this new paradigm, the leaves of the organisational tree – the frontline workers – are likely to be 'digital natives'. They may be highly skilled, degree-educated, constantly learning, and have access to vast amounts of information at their fingertips. They're not a single-use cog in an industrial machine, but dynamic nodes in a living network.

Nature's Value Creators

In a tree, leaves are where the amazing happens. They capture sunlight and convert it into energy for the whole tree. They breathe in carbon dioxide and release oxygen. In short, they are the tree's value creators. They also show the first signs of problems and display the clearest signs of health.

A few years ago, I visited a luxury car dealership. The showroom was impressive, the brand was prestigious, but the experience was terrible. A disengaged salesperson managed to undo millions of pounds in marketing and decades of brand building in just fifteen minutes. Like brown leaves on a tree, their condition told the true story of the organisational health to which they belonged.

Your Living Crown

Your organisation's crown comprises:

- Those who interface directly with customers
- Those who create your products
- Those who deliver your services
- Those who represent your brand to the world

These aren't low-level positions – they're high-value creators (even if the marketplace dictates that they may have low remuneration). Just as leaves create energy for the whole tree, these teams create value for your entire organisation.

Signs of Health

Just as you can instantly assess a tree's health by looking at its leaves, your front-line teams show the true condition of your organisation. A thriving crown manifests through engaged team members, positive customer interactions, consistent quality delivery, innovation and creativity, and proactive problem-solving.

Conversely, just as yellowing leaves signal problems, watch for warning signs in your organisation: high turnover, customer complaints, quality issues, low engagement, and resistance to change.

Supporting Your Crown

Remember, leaves don't support the tree – the tree supports the leaves. Similarly, your front-line teams are not there to support the management, although this may be required from time to time. Management should be supporting them.

🌳 KEY CONCEPT: THE SUPPORTING STRUCTURE

Leaves don't support the tree — the tree supports the leaves. When leaders shift their perspective from "How well are workers serving us?" to "How well are we supporting our value creators?" organisational performance transforms.

I worked with one manufacturing organisation where managers constantly complained about the poor performance of their front-line workers. When I flipped their perspective and asked, "How well are you supporting your value creators?" it led to a change. They began to see their role differently — not as dictators to be served, but as enablers of success stories. This wasn't, of course, instant; it takes a while to authentically value people and naturally think that way.

Resource Flow

Just as leaves need consistent supplies of water and nutrients to function, your front-line teams require essential resources. They need clear information flowing freely, adequate resources to perform their roles well, proper tools for their tasks, ongoing training to develop their skills, regular feedback to guide their growth, and emotional support to maintain their engagement. And, of course, their successful output will feed the tree!

Growth and Adaptation

Watch how leaves respond to sunlight – they move and twist to maximise exposure to opportunity. Your front-line teams need to be similarly positioned. They must be equipped to respond swiftly to market changes, evolving customer needs, and create better solutions for those customers or clients they serve.

The Feedback Loop

Leaves don't just create energy – they send vital information back through the tree about environmental conditions. Your front-line teams should serve as your primary source of market intelligence, customer feedback, operational insights, innovation opportunities, and competitive information. Their direct experience with customers and markets can provide you invaluable insights for the entire organisation.

Creating the Right Environment

Just as leaves need the right conditions to thrive, your value creators require a nurturing environment. This means establishing clear purpose in their work, creating a supportive culture, providing necessary resources, offering development opportunities, and ensuring recognition and appreciation for their contributions. Remember, we all seek identity, worth, value, purpose, security, community, and love.

The Power of the Crown

A healthy crown of leaves creates more than energy. When your front-line teams truly thrive, they naturally attract more opportunities, generate fresh ideas, build stronger relationships with customers, create competitive advantages, and enable sustainable growth for the entire organisation.

Remember also, when a leaf falls from the tree, it lands in the earth and continues to nourish its maker. When your people leave your organisation for whatever reason, do they continue to speak well of it? Do they continue to share with people the positive environment they experienced? Do you carry out exit interviews to try and understand why people are really leaving? Are they leaving your organisation yet remaining great fans of your culture, values, and purpose?

Looking Forward

As you consider your organisation's crown, reflect deeply on how you're treating your value creators. Become clear on who your value creators are. Consider how well you're supporting their success, what might be blocking their effectiveness, and how you could help them thrive even more.

In our next chapter, we'll look at an example of how an organisation may look using the framework of a tree.

Remember: Your front-line teams aren't the bottom of your organisation – they are your crown, your value creators, your face to the world. The whole management structure is there to ensure that they – and therefore your services or products – thrive! When you support them properly, like a tree supports its leaves, they'll transform sunlight into growth for your entire organisation.

9

Organisation Tree Structures

If you look at any traditional organisation chart, the emphasis is on who's running the show, who is responsible, and who the buck stops with. This emphasis makes the whole structure biased towards hierarchy rather than growth. Yet an organisation doesn't exist to create a strong structure; it exists to create a great service or product. Simply turning this upside down changes things. Now, with a tree structure as our framework, this simple illustration points towards the growth of your service or product.

Take the NHS (Healthcare of the UK) as a typical example. Its public organisation charts show who is responsible – row after row of chief medical people, reporting to other chief medical people. The NHS does not exist to create a powerful structure, but to create an enormous network of front-line healthcare professionals – doctors, nurses, surgeons, paramedics, etc. This is the reason the NHS exists. These people, of course, need support and facilities to help them be skilled, efficient, and the best they can be in order to serve the community. For you and me, when we need medical help, the only people we see are the front-line caregivers. We are not interested in the structure that supports them.

When I'm not coaching leaders, I produce a large-scale musical production that I created and co-wrote. It is usually performed by about 20 West End or Broadway actors. On the evening of the performance, the audiences first interaction with the production is the greeting by people who will make them feel welcome and get them efficiently into their seats (Front of House staff). This is the first impression and experience of the show. The audience will then watch these 20 actors deliver their amazing craft. When we perform at large venues, such as Wembley Arena, we have to employ approximately 90 additional people, with functions ranging from lighting, sound, video, rigging, set, costumes, transport, marketing, and many other roles.

In the Inverted Leader model for this organisation, as Producer, I am the trunk. My principal branches would be my Artistic Director, Marketing Director, Musical Director, Front of House Manager, and General Manager. Each of these departmental heads would branch out into their own teams. The actors and Front of House people are the crown on top of this particular tree.

My roots are our accountant, advisors, industry mentors, lawyer, and AV consultants. The whole ecosystem is designed with the sole purpose of putting 20 actors on stage in the best way possible – nothing else.

In this example, who is the most important? Lighting? Without them, the actors won't be seen. Sound? Without them, the actors won't be heard. Writers? Without them, there is nothing to perform. The actors? Obviously, without them, there is no performance. What about marketing? Without ticket sales, we do not have customers; without customers, we have no income. Without income, we cannot put on a performance. So, the truth is, everyone is interdependent. Everyone needs everybody else to do what they do well in order for the public to see, hear, and appreciate the performance being sung. When someone underperforms, the outcome of everyone's work is compromised.

Now, do you think the Front of House people have overheard comments from the audience? They need to feed that back. Do you think the actors have a creative input into how certain phrases could be sung or have introduced their own character traits? Of course! You will often hear of Hollywood actors changing and creating their characters by feeding back their experience and suggestions to the director. The same should go for your organisation. People at the sharp end must have a voice back into the organisation. Your organisation exists only because of what they do.

So, if you draw out your organisation chart now, how about starting with the crown. Start with all the people who will be creating value for your organisation at the top – the people who make the magic that your customers and clients love. Next, consider the kind of support structure that would make them thrive. Also, consider the type of people who would help them thrive. Work down this intricate network of support, ending with your primary branches – the people who will be your trusted limbs. Then of course, the trunk. However, don't stop there. Continue with your roots, your support networks – the anchors and knowledge inputs to the organisation.

What you have created is a complete, healthy structure that is designed for growth.

10

Caring for Your Tree – Health and Maintenance

Reading the Signs

T rees have seasons. Even in winter, an experienced gardener can tell if a tree is healthy. They look for subtle signs – the condition of the bark, the flexibility of young branches, the pattern of bud formation. They know that tomorrow's growth depends on today's health.

The same wisdom applies to organisations. Like a gardener reading the early signs of spring or the first hints of disease, skilled leaders learn to spot subtle changes in their organisation's health. Sometimes, it's as simple as noticing a shift in the energy of morning meetings or a change in how teams interact with each other. Small signs of change in people or their output should alert you to an organisational health issue.

The Whole Living System

When a tree shows signs of distress, simply treating the visible symptoms rarely solves the underlying problem. If leaves are yellowing, the issue might lie in the roots. If branches are failing to thrive, the problem could be in the trunk's transport system.

KEY CONCEPT: TREATING CAUSES, NOT SYMPTOMS

When a tree shows signs of distress, simply addressing visible symptoms rarely solves the underlying problem. If leaves are yellowing, the issue might lie in the roots. Effective leaders look beyond surface issues to find and address root causes.

Very often in my conversations with clients, the issue is rarely the issue. Leaders and managers want to fix what is directly in front of them, but by asking a few questions, we can usually go much deeper and find the root of the real problem. Often, it's not pretty, as more often than not, they themselves are the cause, either directly or indirectly.

Natural Cycles and Rhythms

Not every change signals a problem. Trees go through natural cycles of growth, rest, and renewal. They have seasons of rapid expansion and periods of consolidation. Your organisation may too. Sometimes, what looks like a problem might simply be a natural time of gathering strength before the next phase of growth. It may also signify that some pruning is necessary!

Healing and Recovery

Trees have remarkable healing abilities. Given the right conditions and care, they can recover from significant damage. Your organisation could have this same capacity for renewal. Even after serious setbacks

– like losing key staff or facing market disruption – recovery is possible when you focus on strengthening the core and nurturing new growth.

Growing Stronger Through Challenge

Look closely at a tree that's weathered storms. You'll see how it's grown stronger in response to challenge. The wind that threatens to topple a tree actually stimulates growth that makes it stronger. Similarly, organisations often develop their greatest strengths when facing and overcoming challenges. Relationships (joints) are often strengthened. Innovation may appear, resulting in new growth in a space that was previously empty.

KEY CONCEPT: STRENGTH THROUGH CHALLENGE

Trees that weather storms develop stronger structures in response to stress. The wind that threatens to topple a tree actually stimulates growth, making it more resilient. Organisations often develop their greatest strengths when facing and overcoming challenges, with stronger, improved relationships and innovation emerging in previously unexplored areas.

Looking Forward

As you consider your organisation's health, think about what signs your people are showing you. Where might you need to look deeper than surface symptoms? How could you create conditions that better support natural, healthy growth?

Remember: the healthiest trees aren't those that don't have problems; they're the ones that have developed strength and resilience through proper care and attention to their entire system. Five steps forward and two steps back is a good day!

In our next chapter, we'll explore how to handle major organisational change – the equivalent of transplanting or grafting in the tree world.

11

Disrupt for Growth

The Art of Pruning

One of the most counter-intuitive aspects of tree care is pruning. Sometimes, removing parts of the tree actually promotes overall health. The same principle holds true for organisations.

One of my clients, a furniture manufacturer, experienced this first-hand when reviewing their profitability. Together, we analysed the financial figures across each of their product lines. Through this process, we identified a particular product that generated no profit - and probably never would.

Despite their personal fondness for this item, they made the difficult decision to discontinue it. Resources had been flowing into a part of the business that gave nothing back - effectively draining the organisation of energy and capacity.

This act of pruning allowed more resources to be redirected towards the products that were actually adding value, enabling the entire business to thrive.

KEY CONCEPT: STRATEGIC PRUNING

Counter-intuitively, removing parts of a tree can actually promote its overall health. The same applies to organisations. Discontinuing products or services that drain resources without delivering value allows energy and investment to be redirected to areas that truly contribute.

By letting go of what no longer serves the organisation, you create space for growth where it matters most - enabling the whole business to thrive.

You Need a Transplant

Most of the time, trees grow gradually, adapting slowly to their environment. But sometimes, more dramatic change is required. In the world of trees, this might involve transplanting to new soil or grafting new varieties onto existing rootstock. In an organisation, it might mean relocating to a new area, merging with another business, acquiring a company and integrating it into your existing framework, or completely transforming the way you work.

Any gardener will tell you that transplanting a mature tree is delicate work. The larger the tree, the greater the risk. Roots can be damaged, the tree experiences shock, and recovery takes time. Some trees don't survive the process at all.

One organisation learned this the hard way when expanding their operation into another region of the country. Like a transplanted tree, every part of the organisation felt the impact. The new environment didn't respond in the same way. Informal communication patterns broke down, and even their strongest teams struggled to maintain their previous effectiveness.

The local culture was different. When local people were hired, the working environment changed significantly - including expectations and values. The transplant had not been carried out with sufficient care or consideration, and it proved to be a costly lesson. The attention and care from its leadership ended too soon. It was almost an abdication – the deal was agreed, a plan was made, and the changes were implemented, job done! Except this proved fatal, as it still required their attention, but they had turned their focus on to new things!

The Right Environment

We could also consider the soil in our metaphor. Is the ground you have planted your organisation in fertile? Is it in the right place, and the right conditions to bring life? Have you planted too soon or too late?

How about the weather conditions. Is it dry and harsh? Is it sodden? Are you having to fight against it or can you work with it?

For your organisation to grow successfully, it must be appropriate for the environment in which it exists.

The Grafting Challenge

Sometimes, change means bringing together different parts to create something new. You might be acquiring other organisations and integrating them into your own, or hiring a key figure to lead a division of the business. In the natural world, this is known as grafting - joining one variety onto another's rootstock to combine the best qualities of both.

This process brings its own challenges. The parts must be compatible. The connection point requires careful attention. And even when everything is done correctly, there is still a period of uncertainty while you wait to see if the graft will take.

Supporting Through Transition

During major change, your role as a leader becomes even more crucial. Just as a newly transplanted tree needs extra support, water, and care, your organisation needs strong, stable leadership through the transition.

This is not the time for hands-off management. Like a stake supporting a recently moved tree, your organisation needs visible presence, clear direction, and consistent communication - at least until new roots have established and stability returns.

Expect Some Shock

Even the best-planned changes cause some level of shock to the system. A tree might drop its leaves, show signs of stress, or temporarily pause in growth. Your organisation may display similar symptoms - dips in productivity, increased anxiety, or temporary confusion. This is natural.

KEY CONCEPT: TRANSPLANT SHOCK

Like a transplanted tree that might drop leaves or pause growth, major changes in your organisation will likely show signs of stress during transitions. This does not indicate failure - it is a natural sign of adaptation, requiring extra support and patience.

These early symptoms of strain do not mean the change has failed. They are simply part of the process. The key is to recognise these signs as temporary, while ensuring that the core of the organisation remains strong enough to sustain recovery.

New Growth in New Places

But here's the encouraging part: when a transplant or graft succeeds, the results can be remarkable. Trees often produce new growth in unexpected places. They adapt to new conditions and find new ways to flourish.

The same can happen in organisations. Teams discover more effective ways of working. New opportunities emerge. People develop capabilities they never knew they had.

Protecting What Matters

During major change, it is vital to protect the essential elements of your organisation - your values, your culture, and your key relationships. Like a tree's root ball during transplanting, these core components need careful handling to ensure survival.

Looking Forward

As you contemplate significant change within your organisation, ask yourself: How well have you prepared the ground for transformation? Are your core systems resilient enough to weather the shift? Have you planned in sufficient support to guide your people through the process and beyond?

In the next chapter, we'll explore how to ensure sustainable growth for the future - how to create an organisation that continues to thrive across generations of leadership.

12

Growing Through Generations
The Long View

In the grounds of many English stately homes stand magnificent oak trees that have lived for centuries. They were envisioned by landscape designers who would never live to see them in their full glory. I find that fascinating, like big cathedrals that can take over a century to build – designers, architects and builders creating something for future generations. These oaks have withstood countless storms, witnessed generations of change, and grown stronger with each passing year. In doing so, they have created ecosystems that nurture new life and support everything around them.

Beyond the Single Tree

As organisations mature, they often grow beyond a single structure. Like a grove of trees, they may develop multiple units, divisions, or locations. Each has its own distinct character, while still sharing the same fundamental DNA.

The challenge then becomes not merely maintaining one healthy tree, but nurturing a thriving, interconnected forest.

Passing on Wisdom

Every ring in a tree's trunk tells a story. Each one marks a year of growth, challenge, and adaptation. Similarly, your organisation builds up layers of knowledge and experience over time. The key is ensuring that this wisdom is not lost as people come and go.

I know of many organisations that, over generations, have preserved traditional craftsmanship while embracing new techniques. Like a tree passing nutrients through its network, they have found ways to share knowledge between experienced craftsmen and new apprentices - nurturing continuity while enabling evolution.

Creating Strong Seedlings

Nature ensures its future through seeds - each one containing everything needed to grow a new tree. In organisations, this translates to creating systems and cultures capable of replicating success. It's akin to a franchise model that has perfected a system and can be replicated many times over. It's about building something that carries your values and vision forward, even as leadership changes.

Adapting to New Seasons: The oldest trees have survived by adapting to changing climates while keeping their core strength intact. Today's organisations face similar challenges - emerging technologies, shifting markets, and evolving customer expectations. Success lies in maintaining strong roots while remaining agile enough to adapt to new conditions.

Building Resilient Systems

In a forest, trees don't stand alone. They form complex networks, supporting and nourishing one another through underground fungal connections.

Your organisation needs similar networks - relationships, partnerships, and support systems that enable it to thrive through times of change. These connections strengthen resilience, build collaboration, and ensure the whole system flourishes, not just individual parts.

The Legacy Question

Every leader eventually faces the legacy question: *What will remain after you step away?* The strongest trees create conditions that sustain life long after they're gone. Similarly, truly successful organisations outlive their founders, continuing to grow and adapt through successive generations.

KEY CONCEPT: THE LEGACY QUESTION

The strongest trees create conditions that sustain life long after they're gone. Similarly, truly successful organisations outlive their founders.

What will remain after you step away? Are you building something that can grow and thrive beyond your own leadership? Are you preserving wisdom, nurturing new talent, and creating adaptable systems that will ensure the organisation continues to flourish?

Planning for Tomorrow

Just as a forest requires both ancient trees and new saplings, organisations must balance current stability with future growth. This involves investing in development at all levels: nurturing new talent, exploring new opportunities, and building capabilities for the future.

The Wider Ecosystem

Mature trees don't just sustain themselves; they enrich their entire ecosystem. They provide shelter, create nutrients, and support diverse life forms. Similarly, successful organisations contribute to their broader community, creating more than just profit. When you hear of a large corporation closing down a local facility, the impact is felt much wider than the organisation itself. It send out ripples across their local community affecting their suppliers, and the local economy.

Sustainable Growth

True sustainability isn't simply about survival; it's about creating the conditions for continuous renewal and growth. This means building an organisation that:

- Nurtures new talent naturally
- Adapts to change while maintaining its core strength
- Creates value for all stakeholders
- Contributes positively to its environment

Looking Forward

As you reflect on your organisation's future, consider what you are truly building. Are you creating something that can grow and thrive beyond your own leadership? Are you nurturing the next generation of leaders? Are you developing systems that can adapt and evolve?

Remember: the most successful organisations span generations. They don't just grow; they create the conditions for ongoing renewal and adaptation.

13

Planting Seeds for Change
Beginning Your Journey

Throughout this book, we have explored how nature, particularly trees, can teach us a better way to structure and lead organisations. We have challenged the traditional organisational chart, showing how leadership should support from below rather than control from above. Now, it's time to consider how to put these ideas into practice.

Your journey toward natural, inverted leadership begins wherever you are right now. Perhaps you are leading an established organisation with deeply ingrained traditional structures. Maybe you are starting something new, or perhaps you find yourself somewhere in between, recognising that change is needed but unsure where to begin.

A garden centre owner once shared a piece of wisdom that is perfectly applicable here: "The best time to plant a tree was twenty years ago. The second-best time is today."

Transforming an organisation doesn't happen overnight, just as a seedling doesn't become a mature tree in a season. But small, intentional changes can have lasting and profound effects.

Start by examining your own leadership stance. Are you trying to be the star at the top, or the supportive trunk enabling growth? This simple shift in perspective can change how you and your management team approach every aspect of leadership.

KEY CONCEPT: STARTING TODAY

"The best time to plant a tree was twenty years ago. The second-best time is today." Transformation doesn't happen overnight, however, small, intentional changes can create profound effects over time.

Begin by examining your own leadership stance: Are you trying to be the star at the top, or the supportive trunk enabling growth?

Natural Growth Patterns

Remember, we're not trying to force unnatural change. Just as a tree grows according to its nature and environment, your organisation will find its own way of applying these principles. The key is working with natural patterns, rather than against them.

Moving from Understanding to Action: Consider starting with one area of your organisation. Perhaps begin with a single team or department. Identify who is in the crown, what do they need? Allow this team to experiment with more natural ways of working, supporting risk-taking, and encourage growth (and, by extension, accepting the potential errors and mistakes that come with it!).

The Courage to Change

It takes courage to challenge traditional thinking. When everyone else is drawing industrial-age organisational charts, it's bold to suggest a different way. But nature's wisdom has been proven over millennia. Trees haven't survived this long by accident, they have adapted, sometimes in the most outrageous environments.

Your organisation's transformation should follow a rhythm. Some changes will happen quickly, while others will need time to develop fully. The key is maintaining steady progress while respecting the natural cycles of growth and consolidation.

The Power of Observation

Just as a gardener learns to read the signs of their plants' health, you must develop your ability to observe your organisation's natural patterns. Where is growth happening naturally? Where are resources flowing freely? Where might there be blockages that need your attention?

You may need to start with simply observing, or perhaps you need to free up your time to make observation a priority!

As you implement these changes, think beyond immediate results. You're not just reorganising; you're establishing new patterns that will shape your organisation's growth for years to come. Like planning a forest, consider how today's decisions will affect tomorrow's growth.

Your Next Step

What you're creating isn't just a different type of organisation - it's a living system that can continue growing and adapting long after your time as leader ends. This is perhaps the most powerful aspect of inverted leadership: its ability to create sustainable, ongoing growth.

Consider your immediate next step. It might be as simple as redrawing your organisation chart the right way up, or perhaps it's having a conversation with your team about supporting growth.

Whatever you choose, remember that every natural process starts with a single moment - a seed sprouting, a bud opening, a leaf unfurling. Your journey toward inverted leadership begins with a single action.

There are so many tree types, and nearly every environment has trees that are capable of thriving in it. There will be one that mirrors your organisation and its environment. Try finding one that matches yours.

Final Thoughts

To conclude: Leadership isn't about being at the top of the tree - it's about providing the strong support from which others can grow. When you align your organisation with nature's patterns, you can create something that can truly flourish and last.

In writing this book, I've delved into the biology of trees, and the more I've learned, the more I see the power in creating and growing a lasting organisation based on their ecosystem. Someone once pointed out to me that an X-ray of our lungs is also a picture of a tree, and I can see there the trachea as the trunk - a design that gives us all life and breath.

It was very tempting to be prescriptive in this book and create a 'How-to' manual eg. 3 steps how to do XYZ, or even draw diagrams of what it should look like. However, I feel that just as every person is unique, every organisation is unique, even if it's a duplicate but in a unique environment. Therefore, I wanted it to be a conversation - for every reader to use their imagination, to think of things beyond my own thoughts.

I appreciate that not every single organisation will benefit fully from this framework, however, if your organisation relies on the performance of people, then I believe yours will.

Will you cling to the Industrial Revolution's outdated command-and-control model, or embrace nature's wisdom to build an organisation for globally motivated people that thrives long after your leadership ends?

For further discussion, consultations, speaking engagements or Emotional Intelligence reviews, visit *richardjhaley.com*